A Math Mix-Up

by Stephanie Herbek

HOUGHTON MIFFLIN   BOSTON

PHOTOGRAPHY CREDITS
Cover NASA/JPL-CalTech; **2** NASA/JPL-CalTech

Printed in China

ISBN 10: 0-618-90019-5
ISBN 13: 978-0-618-90019-0

23456789 NOR 16 15 14 13 12 11 10 09 08

It was early in the morning of September 23, 1999. National Aeronautics and Space Administration (NASA) workers in California were carefully watching the Mars Climate Orbiter spacecraft. They were waiting for it to begin making a slow circle—or orbit—around Mars.

The Climate Orbiter spacecraft was worth millions of dollars. Its job was to orbit Mars and gather information, called *data*, about the planet. The data would help scientists understand more about Mars and its weather.

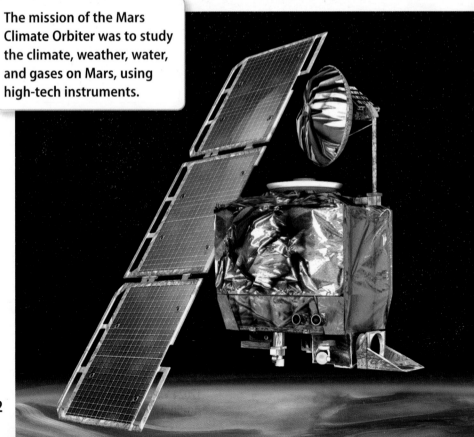

The mission of the Mars Climate Orbiter was to study the climate, weather, water, and gases on Mars, using high-tech instruments.

The spacecraft had been in space for nearly ten months before reaching Mars in September. As it passed behind Mars, everything seemed fine. But NASA waited and waited for Orbiter to come out from behind the planet, and it never did. Where did the spacecraft go? What went wrong?

As soon as the orbiter disappeared, NASA flight controllers in California searched space for it. The company that helped NASA build the Mars Climate Orbiter searched, too. But nobody could find the spacecraft.

Then NASA got some bad news. The missing orbiter had probably exploded and crashed as it circled Mars.

The people at NASA were confused. The orbiter should have been circling about 150 kilometers (93 miles) above Mars. That's what scientists had planned. But the orbiter had actually been flying only 60 kilometers (37 miles) from Mars. That was too close! The orbiter had to remain at least 85 kilometers (53 miles) from Mars to stay safe.

So why was it flying so close to Mars?

Read·Think·Write How far from Mars did NASA expect Orbiter to circle? Give your answer in standard units.

NASA asked a team of workers to figure out what went wrong with the spacecraft. Measurement mistakes had caused the Mars Climate Orbiter to crash!

The orbiter had been controlled by computers on Earth. As NASA workers studied the crash, they found a big problem. The computer programs that controlled the spacecraft used two different kinds of units for measurement: the standard system of measurement including inches, yards, and miles and the metric system of measurement including centimeters, meters, and kilometers. This mix-up was the main reason Orbiter crashed.

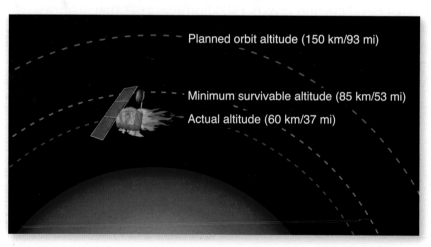

Planned orbit altitude (150 km/93 mi)

Minimum survivable altitude (85 km/53 mi)

Actual altitude (60 km/37 mi)

Because of a math mix-up between the standard and metric systems, Orbiter got too close to Mars.

Today, people use two different systems of measurement.

As Orbiter moved from Earth to Mars, computers often checked its path and changed the way it was flying. Everyone thought the computer programs were using data in metric units. But one of the important programs had been written with data in standard units. The computers had plenty of data about the orbiter, but some of the data were in the wrong units.

The mixed-up data caused the spacecraft to drift off its path. It got closer to Mars than it should have, and crashed.

Standard Units of Length		Metric Units of Length
1 inch	equals	2.54 centimeters
1 yard	equals	0.914 meters
1 mile	equals	1.609 kilometers

Read·Think·Write Is a kilometer more or less than a mile?

With Orbiter, some NASA workers used metric units and some used standard units. Their numbers did not work together because the units were different. Numbers in different units cannot be compared, and math cannot be done correctly unless the same units are used.

Here's a down-to-earth example. Will and Grant want to see who is taller. Will measures his height in inches and finds that he is 50 inches tall. Grant measures his height in centimeters and finds that he is 120 centimeters tall. Who is taller?

You might think that Grant is taller, because his measurement has more units than Will's. But that's not true. Grant measured himself using metric units. Will measured himself using standard units. The boys did not use the same units of measurement, so the number of units cannot be compared.

To compare the heights of the two boys, we must make their units of measurement the same. We can change 50 inches to centimeters by multiplying.

Read·Think·Write If 1 inch = 2.54 centimeters, how many centimeters tall is Will?

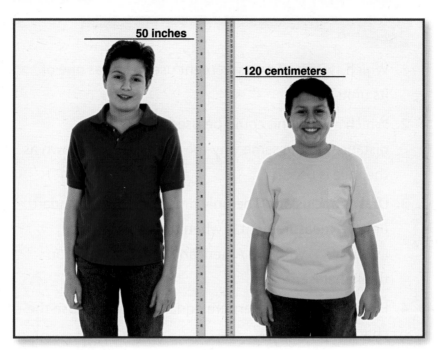

50 inches

120 centimeters

Who is taller?

Using the same units of measurement is very important. The Mars Climate Orbiter crashed because the math that was used to fly it was wrong. If everyone had been using the same units, Orbiter probably would not have crashed. It would have stayed far enough away from Mars to orbit safely and do its job.

Read·Think·Write What unit of measurement would you use to measure each of the following: an ant, a bicycle, distance to Mars?

1. Which system of measurement uses yards as one of its units?

2. Which metric unit could be used to measure distances in the same way the standard unit known as the mile is used?

3. Draw Conclusions The only time NASA uses standard units of measurement is when they are sharing information with the American public. Why do you think that is?

4. How many centimeters are equal to 4 inches? Use the chart on page 5.

Activity

Use a ruler to measure the following objects in both standard and metric units. Make a chart to record the name of each object and its approximate standard and metric measurements.

- your foot
- the height of your desk or table
- your pencil or pen
- the length of a sheet of paper